The Words Know The Way

Joel Lurie Grishaver and Julia Samuels

Prayer	Introduction	Recitation	Word Analysis	Sounding	Comprehension
בָּרְכוּ	1.2	1.3	1.4	1.5	1.6
שְׁמַע	2.2	2.3	2.4	2.5	2.6
מִי-כָמֹכָה	3.2	3.3	3.4	3.5	3.6
קְדוּשָׁה	4.2	4.3	4.4	4.5	4.6
עֹשֶׂה שָׁלוֹם	5.2	5.3	5.4	5.5	5.6
הַדְלָקַת הַנֵּרוֹת	6.2	6.3	6.4	6.5	6.6
הַמּוֹצִיא / הַזָּן אֶת הַכֹּל	7.2	7.3	7.4	7.5	7.6
בּוֹרֵא פְּרִי הַגָּפֶן/הָעֵץ/הָאֲדָמָה	8.2	8.3	8.4	8.5	8.6
שֶׁהֶחֱיָנוּ	9.2	9.3	9.4	9.5	9.6
Four Questions	10.2	10.3	10.4	10.5	10.6

Check off each activity as you complete and master it.

ISBN #0–933873–53–0

Torah Aura Productions
4423 Fruitland Avenue
Los Angeles, California 90058
(800) BE–TORAH
(213) 585–7312

MANUFACTURED IN THE UNITED STATES OF AMERICA

A YOUNG MAN ONCE SNEAKED AWAY FROM HIS FAMILY (WHOM HE LIVED WITH) AND WENT TO SPEND A SHABBAT WITH A GREAT HASIDIC RABBI, THE SEER OF LUBLIN.
THE POWER OF A MINYAN
J. GRIS
LUBLIN
AS SOON AS HE ARRIVED, THE SEER SAID TO HIM:
LEAVE! GO HOME! AND GET THERE BEFORE SHABBAT!
COME AND SPEND SHABBAT WITH US.
COME AND SPEND SHABBAT WITH US.
SURE!
SO THE MAN STARTED FOR HOME, BUT, SOON HE WAS STOPPED.
THEY WENT TO AN INN, JOINED WITH FRIENDS, AND SANG AND DANCED AND PRAYED ALL SHABBAT.
YA
BA
BA
BIM
BAM
RIGHT AFTER SHABBAT, THE SEER SHOWED UP.
I SENT YOU HOME BECAUSE YOU WERE SUPPOSED TO DIE THIS SHABBAT.
BUT... BUT I'M STILL ALIVE?
THE TRUTH IS, A MINYAN IS MORE POWERFUL THAN A WONDER-REBBE. THEY CAN REALLY WORK MIRACLES.

The Call to Worship

When it is time for Moslems to pray, the Muezzin (their prayer leader) goes to the top of a tower and calls the people to worship. All over the city, people bow down and pray.

Jews gather together in synagogues for prayer. When a minyan (at least ten Jews) has assembled, the service leader starts the formal service with the *Barkhu*. Then the congregation answers with its part.

LEADER

בָּרְכוּ אֶת יהוה הַמְבֹרָךְ

Adonai = יהוה

CONGREGATION

בָּרוּךְ יהוה הַמְבֹרָךְ לְעוֹלָם וָעֶד

LEADER

Bless Adonai, The One-Who-Is-Blessed.

CONGREGATION

Blessed Is Adonai, The One-Who-Is-Blessed forever and ever.

Recitation

Read these words:

1. בָּרוּךְ   בָּרְכוּ   יהוה   אֶת
2. הַמְבֹרָךְ   עוֹלָם   לְעוֹלָם   וָעֶד
3. יהוה   הַמְבֹרָךְ   בָּרוּךְ   יהוה
4. בָּרְכוּ   אֶת   יהוה   הַמְבֹרָךְ
5. בָּרוּךְ   יהוה   הַמְבֹרָךְ   בָּרוּךְ
6. לְעוֹלָם   וָעֶד   בָּרְכוּ   וָעֶד

Read these phrases:

7. בָּרְכוּ אֶת יהוה   הַמְבֹרָךְ
8. בָּרוּךְ יהוה הַמְבֹרָךְ   לְעוֹלָם וָעֶד
9. יהוה הַמְבֹרָךְ   בָּרְכוּ אֶת יהוה
10. הַמְבֹרָךְ לְעוֹלָם וָעֶד   בָּרוּךְ יהוה

11. בָּרְכוּ אֶת יהוה הַמְבֹרָךְ
12. בָּרוּךְ יהוה הַמְבֹרָךְ לְעוֹלָם וָעֶד

Word Analysis

Read these words:

1. בָּרְכוּ   בָּרוּךְ   הַמְבֹרָךְ   בְּרָכָה

2. בָּרֵךְ   מְבָרֵךְ   לְבָרֵךְ   בְּרָכוֹת

What do all these words have in common? ______________________

Circle the words which are part of the בָּרוּךְ family.

3. יהוה   אַתָּה   אֱלֹהֵינוּ   בָּרְכוּ   לְעוֹלָם

4. בָּרוּךְ   וָעֶד   אֶת   מְבֹרָךְ   שְׁמַע

5. יִשְׂרָאֵל   בְּרָכָה   בְּרָכוֹת   שָׁלוֹם   שַׁבָּת

6. בָּרְכוּ   אֶת   יהוה   הַמְבֹרָךְ   לְעוֹלָם

7. בָּרוּךְ   יהוה   הַמְבֹרָךְ   לְעוֹלָם   וָעֶד

8. מְבָרֵךְ   לְבָרֵךְ   בָּרֵךְ   הַמְבֹרָךְ   בָּרְכוּ

Bless = [ברך*]

*The בּ and the ב have two different names. They are pronounced differently, too. But, when it comes to Hebrew spelling, one can turn into the other.

Dividing Into Parts

1. בָּ/רְ/כוּ אֶת יהוה הַ/מְ/בֹ/רָךְ

2. בָּ/רוּךְ יהוה הַ/מְ/בֹ/רָךְ לְ/עוֹ/לָם וָ/עֶד

Look at the vowel ◌ְ. What does it tell us about dividing words into parts? ______________

____

Divide these words into parts:

3. שְׁמַע יִשְׂרָאֵל בְּרָכוֹת מְקַדֵּשׁ

4. לְהַדְלִיק מְקַדֵּשׁ לְעוֹלָם מַלְכוּתוֹ

5. כְּבוֹד נֶאְדָּר וְאִמְרוּ מִצְוָה

◌ְ Rules

This vowel ◌ְ is called the *sheva*. It is a very interesting vowel because it does three different things:

1. When the *sheva* is under the first letter of a word it makes a sound like the "a" in the word "about."
2. Almost always, when the *sheva* isn't under the first letter in a word, it has no sound. What the *sheva* does then is end the syllable. Usually, the letter and the vowel before it combine with it to make up the syllable.
3. Sometimes you will find two *shevas* together. When you do, the first one is silent (and ends a syllable) and the second one sounds like a beginning *sheva*.

Reading Clues

*a. Whether it is sounded or silent, a *sheva* usually ends a word part.

*b. Sometimes the *sheva* is combined with another vowel and both of these are placed under one letter. Here it "shortens" the sound of the other vowel. Most of the time you won't notice the difference, but we'll explain how this works later in the book.

Comprehension

בָּרְכוּ אֶת יהוה הַמְבֹרָךְ.

בָּרוּךְ יהוה הַמְבֹרָךְ לְעוֹלָם וָעֶד.

Bless Adonai, The One-Who-Is-Blessed.

Blessed is Adonai, The One-Who-Is-Blessed forever and ever.

1. Circle the Hebrew words which mean "bless."
2. Underline the words which mean "forever and ever."
3. Write the Hebrew word for God's name here: ______________________.

YITZHAK
WHERE DOES GOD LIVE?!
J. GRIS

WHEN RABBI YITZHAK MEIR OF GETZ WAS A LITTLE BOY, HIS MOTHER TOOK HIM TO SEE THE MAGGID OF KOZNITZ.

IN THE WAITING ROOM SOMEONE SAID TO HIM:

I'LL GIVE YOU A GULDEN IF YOU TELL ME WHERE GOD LIVES.

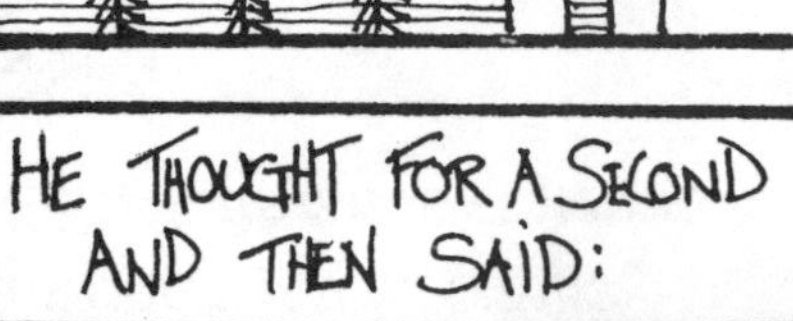
HE THOUGHT FOR A SECOND AND THEN SAID:

I'LL GIVE YOU TWO IF YOU TELL ME WHERE GOD DOESN'T LIVE!

THE MAGGID CAN SEE YOU NOW.

The Watchword of our Faith

The *Shema* comes from the Torah. It is something that God told Moses to teach to the Jewish people. It contains the single most important idea in all of Jewish thought. It reminds us that there is only One God and that all people are connected through our God.

Even though the *Shema* started out as something God said to us, we study it as part of the way we pray. We say the *Shema* when we wake up, when we go to sleep, and when we pray together every morning and evening. The *Shema* teaches an idea we want to live.

שְׁמַע יִשְׂרָאֵל יהוה אֱלֹהֵינוּ יהוה אֶחָד.

בָּרוּךְ שֵׁם כְּבוֹד מַלְכוּתוֹ לְעוֹלָם וָעֶד.

Listen, Israel, Adonai is our God, Adonai is (the) One (God).

Blessed is the Honored Name, His Kingdom is forever and ever.

Recitation

Read these words:

1. שְׁמַע   יִשְׂרָאֵל   יהוה   אֶחָד
2. יהוה   אֱלֹהֵינוּ*   בָּרְכוּ   הַמְבֹרָךְ
3. בָּרוּךְ   שֵׁם   כְּבוֹד   מַלְכוּתוֹ
4. בָּרוּךְ   יהוה   הַמְבֹרָךְ
5. לְעוֹלָם   וָעֶד   לְעוֹלָם   וָעֶד
6. כְּבוֹד   יִשְׂרָאֵל   אֶחָד   מַלְכוּתוֹ

Read these lines:

7. שְׁמַע יִשְׂרָאֵל יהוה אֱלֹהֵינוּ יהוה אֶחָד.
8. בָּרוּךְ שֵׁם כְּבוֹד מַלְכוּתוֹ לְעוֹלָם וָעֶד.
9. בָּרְכוּ אֶת יהוה הַמְבֹרָךְ.
10. בָּרוּךְ יהוה הַמְבֹרָךְ לְעוֹלָם וָעֶד.
11. שְׁמַע יִשְׂרָאֵל   שֵׁם כְּבוֹד מַלְכוּתוֹ
12. יהוה אֶחָד   לְעוֹלָם וָעֶד
13. בָּרוּךְ יהוה הַמְבֹרָךְ   יהוה אֱלֹהֵינוּ
14. מֶלֶךְ הָעוֹלָם   מַלְכוּתוֹ לְעוֹלָם וָעֶד
15. יהוה אֱלֹהֵינוּ יהוה אֶחָד
16. בָּרוּךְ שֵׁם כְּבוֹד מַלְכוּתוֹ לְעוֹלָם וָעֶד

* 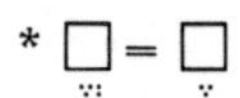

Word Analysis

1. בָּרוּךְ הַמְבֹרָךְ בָּרְכוּ בְּרָכָה

What do all these words have in common?________________________________

2. מַלְכוּתוֹ מֶלֶךְ יִמְלֹךְ מַלְכוּת
3. מַלְכֵּנוּ מַלְכָּה מַלְכֵי כְּמַלְכֵּנוּ

What do all these words have in common?________________________________

Circle the words in the בָּרוּךְ family.

Draw a square around the words in the מֶלֶךְ family.

Clue:
כּ=כ=ךְ

4. אֶחָד מַלְכוּתוֹ כְּבוֹד בָּרְכוּ
5. מֶלֶךְ מַלְכֵי הַמְּלָכִים וָעֶד
6. שְׁמַע הַמְבֹרָךְ מַלְכֵּנוּ בָּרֵךְ
7. אֶת יהוה שֵׁם כְּבוֹד
8. אֵין כֵּאלֹהֵינוּ אֵין מַלְכֵּנוּ
9. בָּרוּךְ אַתָּה מֶלֶךְ הָעוֹלָם

King = מֶלֶךְ

Word Analysis

The words in this exercise come from an ancient hymn of praise to God. For more than 1500 years, it has been a song sung at the end of Shabbat and holiday morning services.

	א	ב	ג	ד
1.	אֵין כֵּאלֹהֵינוּ	אֵין כַּאדוֹנֵינוּ	אֵין כְּמַלְכֵּנוּ	אֵין כְּמוֹשִׁיעֵנוּ
2.	מִי כֵאלֹהֵינוּ	מִי כַאדוֹנֵינוּ	מִי כְמַלְכֵּנוּ	מִי כְמוֹשִׁיעֵנוּ
3.	נוֹדֶה לֵאלֹהֵינוּ	נוֹדֶה לַאדוֹנֵינוּ	נוֹדֶה לְמַלְכֵּנוּ	נוֹדֶה לְמוֹשִׁיעֵנוּ
4.	בָּרוּךְ אֱלֹהֵינוּ	בָּרוּךְ אֲדוֹנֵינוּ	בָּרוּךְ מַלְכֵּנוּ	בָּרוּךְ מוֹשִׁיעֵנוּ
5.	אַתָּה הוּא אֱלֹהֵינוּ	אַתָּה הוּא אֲדוֹנֵינוּ	אַתָּה הוּא מַלְכֵּנוּ	אַתָּה הוּא מוֹשִׁיעֵנוּ

1. The word מֶלֶךְ means __________. All the descriptions of God in column __________ come from the מֶלֶךְ family.
2. The word אֲדֹנָי* is a way of pronouncing God's name יהוה. All the descriptions of God in column __________ call God __________.
3. According to my teacher, the word מוֹשִׁיעַ means __________. It is used in all the descriptions of God found in column __________.
4. The word אֱלֹהִים means God. All the descriptions of God found in column __________ use it.
5. The word-ending נוּ means "our." Circle all of the נוּ endings in this song.

*When a word ends with □ָי, we pronounce it as "aye," just like יהוה.

Comprehension

שְׁמַע יִשְׂרָאֵל יהוה אֱלֹהֵינוּ יהוה אֶחָד.

בָּרוּךְ שֵׁם כְּבוֹד מַלְכוּתוֹ לְעוֹלָם וָעֶד.

Listen Israel, Adonai is our God, Adonai is (the) One (God).

Blessed is the Honored Name, His Kingdom is forever and ever.

1. Underline the words which mean "forever and ever."
2. Circle the word which has to do with blessing.
3. The word מֶלֶךְ means ____________________. Box the word from the מֶלֶךְ family.
4. Copy the Hebrew word which means "Israel" here: ____________________
5. Put two boxes around the Hebrew word which means "One."
6. What is the name of this prayer? ____________________
7. What does the name mean? ____________________ __________

THE MIRACLE OF SINGING
J. GRIS

מִי-כָמֹכָה...

SOMETIMES A PERSON CAN HAVE TROUBLE SINGING ALONE
OH!

BUT CAN SING ALONG WITH ANOTHER PERSON.

THEN THE TWO OF THEM CAN LIFT UP THEIR VOICES AND SING TOGETHER.

RABBI PINHAS OF KORETZ SAID:
THAT IS THE SECRET WHICH BONDS SPIRIT TO SPIRIT

TWEET!

WHEN THE REED SEA WAS DIVIDING, ALL THE ANGELS SANG GOD'S PRAISES, BUT GOD WAS LISTENING TO THE BIRDS.

HOWEVER, WHEN ISRAEL SANG-GOD LISTENED!

RABBI ABRAHAM YAAKOV OF SADAGORA EXPLAINED:

"EVERY ANIMAL HAS ITS OWN SONG. SO DOES EVERY PERSON. ONLY ISRAEL KNOWS HOW TO JOIN THEM ALL

AND SING THEM TO GOD!"

SCOOBIE DO BIM BAM TWEET!

The Song of the Sea

This next prayer is part of the brakhah which follows the *Shema*, called the *G'ulah* (meaning "the redemption*"). This part of the prayer is often called the *Mi Kha-mokhah*, and it is an action adventure.

These words were first sung by the Jewish people right after the Reed Sea divided and miraculously allowed them to cross safely, escaping from Egypt. This song expressed their joy at being saved, at being free.

When we pray these words, we go back to that moment and remember the feeling of being redeemed from slavery. It gives us hope that with God's help, we can redeem the whole world.

מִי־כָמֹכָה בָּאֵלִם, יהוה.
מִי־כָּמֹכָה נֶאְדָּר בַּקֹּדֶשׁ,
נוֹרָא תְהִלֹּת, עֹשֵׂה פֶלֶא.

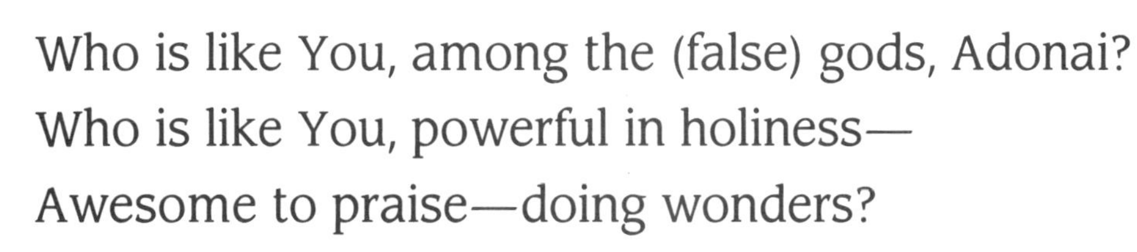

Who is like You, among the (false) gods, Adonai?
Who is like You, powerful in holiness—
Awesome to praise—doing wonders?

יהוה יִמְלֹךְ לְעוֹלָם וָעֶד.

Adonai will rule forever and ever.

בָּרוּךְ אַתָּה יהוה, גָּאַל יִשְׂרָאֵל.

Blessed are You, Adonai, the One-Who-Redeemed Israel.

* Redemption means making the world better.

Recitation

Read these words:

1. נוֹרָא יִמְלֹךְ *גָּאַל יִשְׂרָאֵל
2. כָּמֹכָה בַּקֹּדֶשׁ *עֹשֵׂה פֶלֶא
3. לְעוֹלָם וָעֶד *נֶאְדָּר *תְּהִלֹּת
4. בָּאֵלִם כָּמֹכָה יהוה אַתָּה
5. בָּרוּךְ כְּבוֹד שְׁמַע הַמְבֹרָךְ
6. כָּמֹכָה *נֶאְדָּר *תְּהִלֹּת יִשְׂרָאֵל

Read these phrases:

7. מִי כָמֹכָה לְעוֹלָם וָעֶד בָּאֵלִם יהוה
8. נֶאְדָּר בַּקֹּדֶשׁ יהוה יִמְלֹךְ גָּאַל יִשְׂרָאֵל
9. נוֹרָא תְהִלֹּת מִי כָּמֹכָה עֹשֵׂה פֶלֶא
10. בָּרוּךְ שֵׁם כְּבוֹד מַלְכוּתוֹ לְעוֹלָם וָעֶד.
11. יהוה יִמְלֹךְ לְעוֹלָם וָעֶד.
12. מִי כָּמֹכָה נֶאְדָּר בַּקֹּדֶשׁ,
13. נוֹרָא תְהִלֹּת, עֹשֵׂה פֶלֶא
14. בָּרוּךְ אַתָּה יהוה, גָּאַל יִשְׂרָאֵל.
15. מִי כָמֹכָה בָּאֵלִם, יהוה.

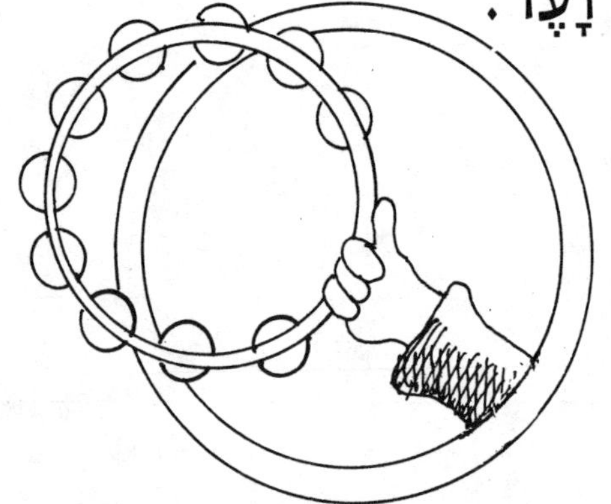

* All of the strange dots are explained on page 3.5

Word Analysis

אֱלֹהִים מִי כֵּאלֹהֵינוּ מִי כַּאדוֹנֵינוּ אֲדֹנָי

מֶלֶךְ מִי כְּמַלְכֵּנוּ מִי כְּמוֹשִׁיעֵנוּ מוֹשִׁיעַ

What do these four phrases have in common? ______________________________

With your teacher's help, explain these three language parts:

מִי = ____________________

כַּ□□□ (כְּ/כֵּ/כָּ) = ____________________

□□□נוּ = ____________________

מִי כָמֹכָה בָּאֵלִם יהוה.

1. The two letters אֵל mean God. (Circle) the word with those two letters.
2. [Box] the word which means "who."
3. God's name is ______________________________
4. Explain the word כָמֹכָה: ______________________________

____

Sounding Clues

The Dagesh

A. Name these Hebrew letters: פ פּ כ כּ ב בּ

B. The dot found inside פּ, כּ, and בּ is called a *dagesh*. What does the *dagesh* do to these letters?

____

C. The *dagesh* can also be found in most other Hebrew letters, but here it doesn't change the way the letter is pronounced.

Circle the letters whose sound is changed by the *dagesh*:

1. דּ לּ מּ גּ בּ הּ שּׁ פּ סּ קּ

2. זּ כּ צּ יּ תּ טּ נּ שּׁ לּ בּ

D. Often the *dagesh* tells you that a letter's sound needs to be doubled. The rules of when that happens are too complex to learn right now. You'll learn about it later in your Hebrew career.

The Double-Duty Dot

A. If you looked at the word עֹשֶׂה and were confused by the שׂ˙, that is okay. It is confusing. We don't know at first glance if the letter is a שׁ or a שׂ.

(The truth: שׂ˙ = שׂוֹ)

B. On the other hand, read this name: מֹשֶׁה

You know this person, even though you might expect his name to be written like this: מוֹשֶׁה. Here the dot has done double duty, being both the dot on the שׁ and the vowel וֹ. This is another thing practice will help your recognize.

Dividing Into Parts

Break these words into parts:

1. נֶאְ/דָּר   בַּ/קֹ/דֶשׁ   פֶ/לֶא   נוֹ/רָא
2. מִי   יִמְלֹךְ   וָעֶד   עֹשֵׂה
3. תְהִלֹּת   גָּאַל   בָּרוּךְ   כָּמֹכָה
4. בָּאֵלִם   יִשְׂרָאֵל   אַתָּה   כָּמֹכָה

3.6

Comprehension

מִי־כָמֹכָה בָּאֵלִם, יהוה.
מִי־כָמֹכָה נֶאְדָּר בַּקֹּדֶשׁ,
נוֹרָא תְהִלֹּת, עֹשֵׂה פֶלֶא.

Who is like You, among the (false) gods, Adonai?
Who is like You, powerful in holiness—
Awesome to praise—doing wonders?

יהוה יִמְלֹךְ לְעוֹלָם וָעֶד.

Adonai will rule forever and ever.

בָּרוּךְ אַתָּה יהוה, גָּאַל יִשְׂרָאֵל.

Blessed are You, Adonai, the One-Who-Redeemed Israel.

1. Underline the phrases which mean "Who is like You . . . . "
2. Double underline the phrase which means "forever and ever."
3. Copy God's name on this line: ____________________
4. Box the word which means "God" (and uses אֵל).
5. According to my teacher, ________ means "holy." Double box the word which includes it.

HOW HEAVY is HOLY
J. GRIS

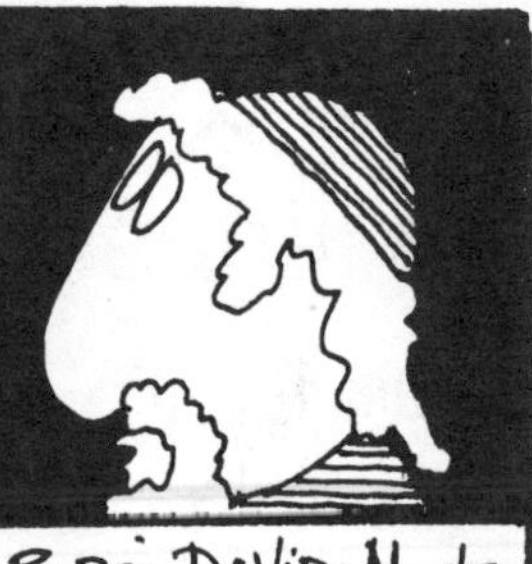
RABBI DAVID MOSHE OF TCHORTIKOV WAS NOT A BIG MAN.

ONCE, WHEN A HEAVY NEW TORAH WAS DEDICATED, HE HAD TO HOLD IT FOR A LONG, LONG TIME.

AFTER A WHILE A BIG MAN ASKED
DO YOU WANT ME TO TAKE OVER?

HE ANSWERED:
NO!
THE HOLY ARK-&-THE-COVENANT WAS VERY HEAVY. IT WAS ALMOST IMPOSSIBLE TO LIFT.

BUT ONCE IT WAS LIFTED, IT CARRIED THE MEN WHO LIFTED IT.

ONCE YOU HOLD SOMETHING HOLY, IT ISN'T HEAVY ANYMORE!

OH!

The Holiness

When Abraham comes to the Land of Israel, the Torah tells us, "Adonai was seen by him." People don't often get to see God. Jacob, Abraham's grandson, dreamed of angels and even wrestled with angels, but probably never got to see God. When Moses dies, the Torah tells us, "he was the only prophet who knew God face to face."

Isaiah was a prophet. He came as close to seeing God as anyone except for Moses (and maybe Abraham and Jacob). One day he went into the Temple in Jerusalem and saw a lot of angels and what was probably the bottom of God's throne. The words of the *Kedushah* come from his vision. They are at the heart of the *Amidah*, the silent prayer. The *Kedushah* is the time during the service when we feel closest to God.

קָדוֹשׁ, קָדוֹשׁ, קָדוֹשׁ יהוה צְבָאוֹת,
מְלֹא כָל־הָאָרֶץ כְּבוֹדוֹ.

Holy, Holy, Holy is Adonai of Hosts,

The whole earth is full of His honor.

יִמְלֹךְ יהוה לְעוֹלָם, אֱלֹהַיִךְ צִיּוֹן לְדֹר וָדֹר, הַלְלוּיָהּ.

Adonai will rule forever, Your God, Zion,

from generation to generation, Halleluyah!

בָּרוּךְ אַתָּה יהוה, הָאֵל הַקָּדוֹשׁ.

Blessed be You, Adonai, the Holy God.

Recitation

Read these words:

1. נֶאְדָּר   בַּקֹּדֶשׁ   הַקָּדוֹשׁ   קָדוֹשׁ
2. יהוה   יִמְלֹךְ   צְבָאוֹת   לְעוֹלָם
3. הָאֵל   אֱלֹהֵינוּ   אֱלֹהַיִךְ   אַתָּה
4. צִיּוֹן   לְדֹר   וָדֹר   הָאָרֶץ
5. כְּבוֹד   כְּבוֹדוֹ   צְבָאוֹת   הַלְלוּיָהּ
6. *כָּל   מְלֹא   קָדוֹשׁ   הַקָּדוֹשׁ

Read these phrases:

7. קָדוֹשׁ, קָדוֹשׁ, קָדוֹשׁ   הָאֵל הַקָּדוֹשׁ   בָּרוּךְ אַתָּא יהוה
8. לְדֹר וָדֹר   מְלֹא כָל־הָאָרֶץ   יהוה צְבָאוֹת
9. כָּל־הָאָרֶץ כְּבוֹדוֹ   הַלְלוּיָהּ   גָּאַל יִשְׂרָאֵל
10. יִמְלֹךְ יהוה לְעוֹלָם   נוֹרָא תְהִלֹּת   אֱלֹהַיִךְ צִיּוֹן
11. קָדוֹשׁ, קָדוֹשׁ, קָדוֹשׁ יהוה צְבָאוֹת, מְלֹא כָל־הָאָרֶץ כְּבוֹדוֹ.
12. יִמְלֹךְ יהוה לְעוֹלָם, אֱלֹהַיִךְ צִיּוֹן לְדֹר וָדֹר, הַלְלוּיָהּ.
13. בָּרוּךְ אַתָּה יהוה, הָאֵל הַקָּדוֹשׁ.

*כָּל = כוֹל. ◌ָ is a *kammatz katan*. It is explained on page 25.

Word Analysis

Read all these words:

1. קָדוֹשׁ   קָדִישׁ   קְדֻשָּׁה   קָדוֹשׁ

2. בַּקֹּדֶשׁ   הַקָּדוֹשׁ   נְקַדֵּשׁ   קֹדֶשׁ

Holy = [קדשׁ]

What do you notice? ______________________________

1. Read the words below. 2. Circle the words in the קָדוֹשׁ family. 3. Box the words in the מֶלֶךְ faimly. 4. Underline the words in the בָּרוּךְ family.

3. שֵׁם   צְבָאוֹת   מֶלֶךְ   עָלֵינוּ

4. מַלְכוּתוֹ   הַלְלוּיָהּ   בָּרְכוּ   אֶת

5. לְדֹר   בְּרָכָה   הָאָרֶץ   מֶלֶךְ

6. בַּקֹּדֶשׁ   הַמְבֹרָךְ   צִיּוֹן   קָדוֹשׁ

7. כָּל   מַלְכֵּנוּ   הָאֵל   יִמְלֹךְ

8. בָּרוּךְ   יהוה   הַקָּדוֹשׁ   קְדֻשָּׁה

Word Surgery

The word "Halleluyah" in English comes directly from the Hebrew הַלְלוּיָהּ.
The Hebrew word הַלֵּל means "praise."

God's Hebrew name is________________.

הַלְלוּיָהּ means "praise God." Can you find where that word mentions God?

Sounding

Kammatz Katan

Sometimes the vowel ◌ָ is pronounced like an וֹ and not an ◌ַ. When that happens, it is called a *kammatz katan*. In this book, we will print every ◌ָ *kammatz katan* a little larger than an ordinary ◌ָ, and it will be easy for you to recognize them. Some siddurim also do this.

Kammatz katan means "a short *kammatz*." A regular *kammatz* makes an "ah" sound. A *kammatz katan* makes an "awe" sound. According to people who study languages, an "awe" is a short "ah."

There are some very complicated rules for knowing when to say a *kammatz katan, but it is not important for you to learn them right now.*

Ḥataf Kammatz

Remember the vowel ◌ְ? We learned that sometimes it can be combined with other vowels under the same letter. When this happens, it "shortens" their sound. Now is the time for us to explain what that means.

The ◌ְ can be combined with three vowels: ◌ֲ, ◌ֱ, and ◌ֳ.

◌ֲ = ◌ַ and ◌ֱ = ◌ֶ. It is only with ◌ֳ that we can hear the difference. ◌ֳ = a short *kammatz* (a *kammatz katan*) and is pronounced "awe" instead of "ah."

Dividing Into Parts

Break the קְדֻשָּׁה into parts. Circle every *kammatz katan* you find.

1. קָדוֹשׁ, קָדוֹשׁ, קָדוֹשׁ יהוה צְבָאוֹת, מְלֹא כָל־הָאָרֶץ כְּבוֹדוֹ.

2. יִמְלֹךְ יהוה לְעוֹלָם, אֱלֹהַיִךְ צִיּוֹן לְדֹר וָדֹר, הַלְלוּיָהּ.

3. בָּרוּךְ אַתָּה יהוה, הָאֵל הַקָּדוֹשׁ.

Comprehension

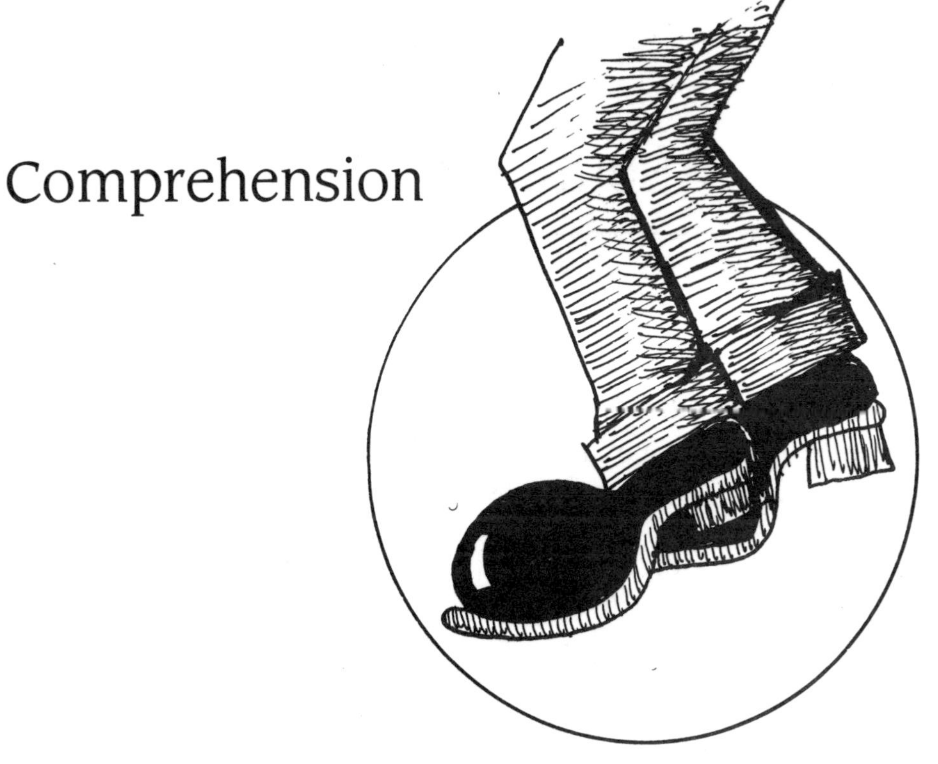

קָדוֹשׁ, קָדוֹשׁ, קָדוֹשׁ יהוה צְבָאוֹת,
מְלֹא כָל־הָאָרֶץ כְּבוֹדוֹ.

Holy, Holy, Holy is Adonai of Hosts,

The whole earth is full of His honor.

יִמְלֹךְ יהוה לְעוֹלָם, אֱלֹהַיִךְ צִיּוֹן לְדֹר וָדֹר, הַלְלוּיָהּ.

Adonai will rule forever, Your God, Zion,

from generation to generation, Halleluyah!

בָּרוּךְ אַתָּה יהוה, הָאֵל הַקָּדוֹשׁ.

Blessed be You, Adonai, the Holy God.

1. Circle all the words in the קָדוֹשׁ family. קָדוֹשׁ means ____________________
2. Box God's name. Also box God's name in "halleluyah."
3. Underline the Hebrew word for "forever."
4. Double underline the Hebrew words for "generation to generation."

THE PEACE PUDDING
J. GRIS.
A HUSBAND AND WIFE CAME TO SEE THE MAGGID OF KOZNITZ
I WORK HARD ALL WEEK. ON SHABBAT I WANT MY PUDDING!

BUT MY WIFE SERVES IT LAST, AFTER THE FISH, THE SOUP, THE CHICKEN, AND EVERYTHING!

AFTER I EAT ALL THAT, THERE IS NO ROOM FOR THE PUDDING.
I WANT MY PUDDING!
SHE WON'T SERVE IT FIRST!
RIGHT! NO WAY!
IT IS WRONG TO SERVE DESSERT FIRST. I WON'T DO IT.
THEN THE MAGGID GAVE HIS ANSWER:
SHALOM BAYIT, FAMILY PEACE, IS THE MOST IMPORTANT THING.

FROM NOW ON, MAKE 2 PUDDINGS EACH SHABBAT. SERVE 1 BEFORE DINNER AND 1 AFTER IT.
THEY TOOK HIS ADVICE AND LIVED HAPPILY.
FROM THEN ON, THE MAGGID'S WIFE MADE 2 PUDDINGS EACH AND EVERY SHABBAT, TOO!

The Peacemaker

The words on this page are a popular Hebrew song—actually, there are several songs set to these words, and I bet you know at least one. That's because the sentence which follows is one of the most popular lines in all of Hebrew prayer. It is a request for peace.

This very sentence is used both at the end of the *Kaddish*, a prayer which says that God is holy, and *Birkat Ha-mazon*, the brakhot said after eating. Prayers for peace also end the *Amidah*, the silent prayer, and the blessing of the priests. Peace is the most important brakhah we can receive.

עֹשֶׂה שָׁלוֹם בִּמְרוֹמָיו,
הוּא יַעֲשֶׂה שָׁלוֹם עָלֵינוּ וְעַל כָּל־יִשְׂרָאֵל,
וְאִמְרוּ אָמֵן.

The One-Who-Makes peace in His heavens—
He will make peace for us and for all Israel,
and say Amen.

Recitation

Read these words:

1. עֹשֶׂה יַעֲשֶׂה יִשְׂרָאֵל שָׁלוֹם
2. בִּמְרוֹמָיו וְעַל וְאִמְרוּ הוּא
3. קָדוֹשׁ כָּל הַמְבֹרָךְ גָּאַל
4. *עָלֵינוּ יִמְלֹךְ כָמֹכָה לְעוֹלָם
5. נוֹרָא נֶאְדָּר וָעֶד כְּמוֹשִׁיעֵנוּ
6. צְבָאוֹת אֵין אַתָּה אָמֵן

Read these phrases:

7. עֹשֶׂה שָׁלוֹם בִּמְרוֹמָיו   שְׁמַע יִשְׂרָאֵל יהוה אֱלֹהֵינוּ
8. מִי כָמֹכָה בָּאֵלִם   הוּא יַעֲשֶׂה שָׁלוֹם עָלֵינוּ
9. בָּרְכוּ אֶת יהוה הַמְבֹרָךְ   נֶאְדָּר בַּקֹּדֶשׁ
10. וְעַל כָּל־יִשְׂרָאֵל   יהוה יִמְלֹךְ לְעֹלָם וָעֶד
11. בָּרוּךְ אַתָּה יהוה, הָאֵל הַקָּדוֹשׁ   נוֹרָא תְהִלֹּת, עֹשֵׂה פֶלֶא
12. עֹשֶׂה שָׁלוֹם בִּמְרוֹמָיו   הוּא יַעֲשֶׂה שָׁלוֹם
13. עָלֵינוּ וְעַל כָּל־יִשְׂרָאֵל   וְאִמְרוּ אָמֵן

*When a י follows the vowel □ֵי or □ֶי, it is silent.

Word Analysis

Read these words:

1. עֹשֶׂה   יַעֲשֶׂה   עוֹשֶׂה   נַעֲשֶׂה

What do they all have in common? ______________________________

Draw a line connecting members of the same family.

2.

מֶלֶךְ	יַעֲשֶׂה
עֹשֶׂה	בָּרְכוּ
בָּרוּךְ	הַקָּדוֹשׁ
קָדוֹשׁ	יִמְלֹךְ

1. Circle the words in the עֹשֶׂה family. 2. Box words in the מֶלֶךְ family.
3. Underline words in the קָדוֹשׁ family. 4. Double underline words in the בָּרוּךְ family.

3.	שֵׁם	מַלְכוּתוֹ	עָלֵינוּ	יַעֲשֶׂה
4.	כְּבוֹד	עוֹשֶׂה	יִשְׂרָאֵל	בַּקֹּדֶשׁ
5.	עֹשֶׂה	הַמְבֹרָךְ	בָּרוּךְ	יִמְלֹךְ
6.	קָדוֹשׁ	בָּאֵלִם	הָאֵל	כָּל
7.	יַעֲשֶׂה	מֶלֶךְ	בָּרְכוּ	אֱלֹהַיִךְ
8.	הָאָרֶץ	וָעֶד	מַלְכֵּנוּ	תְּהִלֹּת

[עשה] = make/do

Dividing Into Parts

Divide the words in עֹשֶׂה שָׁלוֹם into parts:

1. עֹשֶׂה שָׁלוֹם בִּמְרוֹמָיו,
2. הוּא יַעֲשֶׂה שָׁלוֹם עָלֵינוּ וְעַל כָּל־יִשְׂרָאֵל,
3. וְאִמְרוּ אָמֵן.

Relatives

What do these words have in common?

4. הָאֵל אֱלֹהֵינוּ כֵּאלֹהֵינוּ בָּאֵלִם

5. עַל עָלֵינוּ וְעַל

6. תְּהִלֹּת הַלְלוּיָהּ

7. כְּבוֹד כְּבוֹדוֹ

Comprehension

עֹשֶׂה שָׁלוֹם בִּמְרוֹמָיו,
הוּא יַעֲשֶׂה שָׁלוֹם עָלֵינוּ וְעַל כָּל־יִשְׂרָאֵל,
וְאִמְרוּ אָמֵן.

The One-Who-Makes peace in His heavens—
He will make peace for us and for all Israel,
and say Amen.

1. Underline the words in the עֹשֶׂה family.
2. Copy the Hebrew word for "peace" here: ____________________
3. Copy the Hebrew word for "Israel" here: ____________________
4. A "נוּ" ending means ____________________. Circle all of them.
5. The word עַל means "on." It appears twice in this prayer, both times as part of a complex word. Box both of them.
6. Circle the one *kammatz katan* in this prayer. It is in the word ____________, which means "all."

LIGHT
WHEN THEY WERE FIRST MARRIED, RABBI MOSHE EFRAIM AND SARAH WERE VERY HAPPY AND VERY VERY POOR.
THEY WERE SO POOR THAT SARAH HAD TO MAKE HER OWN SHABBAT CANDLESTICKS OUT OF CLAY.
LATER THEY BECAME RICH AND ONE OF THE FIRST THINGS THE RABBI DID WAS BUY SARAH A SILVER CANDELABRA.
DOESN'T EVERYTHING LOOK BRIGHT NOW!
MY LOVE, EVERY SHABBAT YOU HAVE MADE HAS LOOKED BRIGHT TO ME.
AND THEY LIVED VERY VERY VERY HAPPILY EVER AFTER.

The Mitzvah of Lighting

Most Jewish holidays begin twice. They begin when the candles are kindled and blessed, and then again when the *kiddush* is said over the wine. Both of these brakhot help us to recognize the holiness of Shabbat or the festival, and to make it part of our experience.

Kindling lights to mark the beginning of Shabbat or a festival, and or for lighting the H̱anukkah Menorah is a *mitzvah*. It is something we are commanded to do. Each of these acts of lighting a flame is an opportunity—a chance to kindle a feeling of holiness inside ourselves.

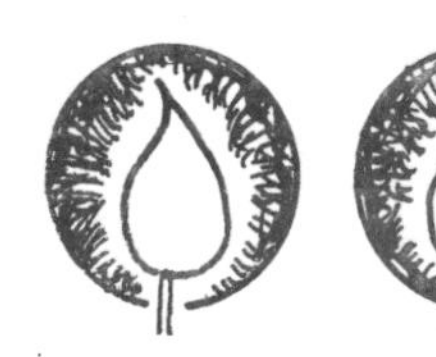

בָּרוּךְ אַתָּה יהוה אֱלֹהֵינוּ מֶלֶךְ הָעוֹלָם,
אֲשֶׁר קִדְּשָׁנוּ בְּמִצְוֹתָיו וְצִוָּנוּ
לְהַדְלִיק נֵר שֶׁל שַׁבָּת.

Blessed are You, Adonai, Ruler of the Cosmos,
Who makes us holy with His mitzvot and made it a mitzvah for us
to kindle the Shabbat light.

בָּרוּךְ אַתָּה יהוה אֱלֹהֵינוּ מֶלֶךְ הָעוֹלָם,
אֲשֶׁר קִדְּשָׁנוּ בְּמִצְוֹתָיו וְצִוָּנוּ
לְהַדְלִיק נֵר שֶׁל יוֹם טוֹב.

Blessed are You, Adonai, Ruler of the Cosmos,
Who makes us holy with His mitzvot and made it a mitzvah for us
to kindle the Festival light.

בָּרוּךְ אַתָּה יהוה אֱלֹהֵינוּ מֶלֶךְ הָעוֹלָם,
אֲשֶׁר קִדְּשָׁנוּ בְּמִצְוֹתָיו וְצִוָּנוּ
לְהַדְלִיק נֵר שֶׁל חֲנֻכָּה.

Blessed are You, Adonai, Ruler of the Cosmos,
Who makes us holy with His mitzvot and made it a mitzvah for us
to kindle the H̱anukkah light.

Recitation

Read these words:

1. בָּרוּךְ נֵר מֶלֶךְ *בְּמִצְוֹתָיו
2. שֶׁל וְצִוָּנוּ אֲשֶׁר לְהַדְלִיק
3. יוֹם חֲנֻכָּה קִדְּשָׁנוּ טוֹב
4. שַׁבָּת אֱלֹהֵינוּ הָעוֹלָם אַתָּה
5. הַמְבָרֵךְ יַעֲשֶׂה יהוה אָמֵן
6. כָמֹכָה הוּא תְּהִלֹּת שָׁלוֹם

Read these phrases:

7. בָּרוּךְ אַתָּה יהוה אֱלֹהֵינוּ מֶלֶךְ הָעוֹלָם
8. אֲשֶׁר קִדְּשָׁנוּ בְּמִצְוֹתָיו וְצִוָּנוּ לְהַדְלִיק
9. נֵר שֶׁל שַׁבָּת נֵר שֶׁל יוֹם טוֹב
10. עֹשֶׂה שָׁלוֹם בִּמְרוֹמָיו מִי־כָמֹכָה בָּאֵלִם יהוה
11. נֵר שֶׁל חֲנֻכָּה שְׁמַע יִשְׂרָאֵל

*תָיו = תָו

We will explain how מִצְוֹתָיו = מִצְווֹתָיו on page 37.

Word Analysis

1. מִצְוָה מִצְוֹת וְצִוָּנוּ צַו
2. בְּמִצְוֹתָיו מִצְוֹתֶיךָ מִצְוַת מְצַוְּךָ

What do all these words have in common? ______________________

1. Circle the words in מִצְוָה family.
2. Box the words in the עֹשֶׂה family.
3. Underline the words in the מֶלֶךְ family.
4. Double underline the words in the בָּרוּךְ family.
5. Star the words in the קָדוֹשׁ family.

3. מְבֹרָךְ שָׁלוֹם יִמְלֹךְ אֶחָד צַו
4. בַּקֹּדֶשׁ בָּרוּךְ עָלֵינוּ מֶלֶךְ עֹשֶׂה
5. יַעֲשֶׂה שְׁמַע בָּרְכוּ בְּמִצְוֹתָיו מַלְכֵּנוּ
6. וְצִוָּנוּ כָּל קָדוֹשׁ מְבָרֵךְ מַעֲשֶׂה
7. שֵׁם מִצְוֹת יִמְלֹךְ נַעֲשֶׂה בְּרָכָה
8. מִצְוַת בַּקֹּדֶשׁ בְּרָכוֹת מַלְכוּתוֹ הַקָּדוֹשׁ

[צוה]* = command

*Note on the ה. When the ה is the last letter of the "base-word," it sometimes falls off.

Sounding

Two Vavs in One

ו—This is a Hebrew letter named "vav." It makes a "v" sound.

וֹ—This is a Hebrew vowel which makes an "o" sound and which is called a *holam*.

וֹ—This could be one of two different things. It could just be a vowel which makes an "o" sound. Or it could be a "vav" with a vowel, which together make a "vo" sound.

The rule which helps you tell the difference is simple. If the letter before the וֹ has a vowel, then the וֹ says "vo." Otherwise it just says "o."

Read these words. Underline the ones where the וֹ says "vo."

1. קָדוֹשׁ מִצְוֹת מִצְוָה עֲוֹנָה

2. עָוֹן בְּמִצְוֹת עוֹשֶׂה כְּמוֹשִׁיעֵנוּ

Read these brakhot:

3. בָּרְכוּ אֶת יהוה הַמְבֹרָךְ.

4. בָּרוּךְ יהוה הַמְבֹרָךְ לְעוֹלָם וָעֶד.

5. בָּרוּךְ שֵׁם כְּבוֹד מַלְכוּתוֹ לְעוֹלָם וָעֶד.

6. בָּרוּךְ אַתָּה יהוה, גָּאַל יִשְׂרָאֵל.

7. בָּרוּךְ אַתָּה יהוה, הָאֵל הַקָּדוֹשׁ.

8. בָּרוּךְ אַתָּה יהוה, הַמְבָרֵךְ אֶת־עַמּוֹ יִשְׂרָאֵל בַּשָּׁלוֹם.

9. בָּרוּךְ אַתָּה יהוה אֱלֹהֵינוּ מֶלֶךְ הָעוֹלָם, אֲשֶׁר קִדְּשָׁנוּ בְּמִצְוֹתָיו וְצִוָּנוּ לְהַדְלִיק נֵר שֶׁל שַׁבָּת.

10. בָּרוּךְ אַתָּה יהוה אֱלֹהֵינוּ מֶלֶךְ הָעוֹלָם, אֲשֶׁר קִדְּשָׁנוּ בְּמִצְוֹתָיו וְצִוָּנוּ לְהַדְלִיק נֵר שֶׁל יוֹם טוֹב.

11. בָּרוּךְ אַתָּה יהוה אֱלֹהֵינוּ מֶלֶךְ הָעוֹלָם, אֲשֶׁר קִדְּשָׁנוּ בְּמִצְוֹתָיו וְצִוָּנוּ לְהַדְלִיק נֵר שֶׁל חֲנֻכָּה.

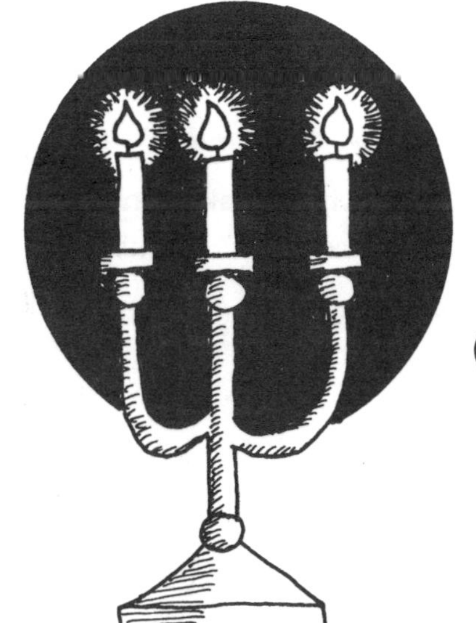

6.6

Comprehension

בָּרוּךְ אַתָּה יהוה אֱלֹהֵינוּ מֶלֶךְ הָעוֹלָם,
אֲשֶׁר קִדְּשָׁנוּ בְּמִצְוֹתָיו וְצִוָּנוּ . . .

Blessed are You, Adonai, Ruler of the Cosmos,
Who makes us holy with His mitzvot and made it a mitzvah for us . . .

to kindle the Shabbat light.	לְהַדְלִיק נֵר שֶׁל שַׁבָּת.
to kindle the Festival light.	לְהַדְלִיק נֵר שֶׁל יוֹם טוֹב.
to kindle the Hanukkah light.	לְהַדְלִיק נֵר שֶׁל חֲנֻכָּה.

1. Circle the Hebrew words for Shabbat, Hanukkah, and Festival.
2. Box the words from the מִצְוָה family.
3. The word קָדוֹשׁ means ________________. Underline the compound word which includes קָדוֹשׁ.
4. The ending on the קָדוֹשׁ word is ________________. It means ________________.
5. Double underline the word which means "light."

TWO BEST FRIENDS USED TO SPEND SHABBAT WITH THE RABBI OF ROPTCHITZ.

THE LESSON OF THE LOAVES

J. GRIS

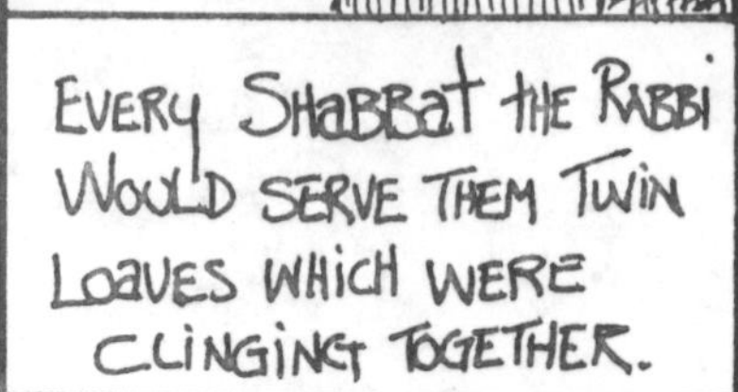

EVERY SHABBAT THE RABBI WOULD SERVE THEM TWIN LOAVES WHICH WERE CLINGING TOGETHER.

ONE WEEK THE TWO OF THEM HAD A FIGHT AND THEY STOPPED TALKING TO EACH OTHER.

THEY WERE STILL ANGRY WHEN THEY CAME TO SHABBAT DINNER

BEFORE SERVING THEM, THE RABBI TOOK A **KNIFE** AND CUT THE LOAVES APART.

RIGHT AFTER DINNER THE TWO EX-FRIENDS FELT THE NEED TO TALK.

BY THE NEXT SHABBAT THE TWO FRIENDS WERE AGAIN BEST FRIENDS.

AND THE RABBI AGAIN SERVED THEM A SIAMESE-HALLAH.

The Pleasure of Eating

For Jews, it is a mitzvah to say a brakhah both before and after eating. In the Torah God tells Moses to teach us: "When you have *eaten* and you are *nourished*, you should *bless* Adonai, your God." Deuteronomy 8.10 That sentence teaches us that we should say a brakhah after eating. The idea that we should also say one before eating was our own; the rabbis of the Talmud came up with the idea.

For Jews, a meal includes bread. We say the brakhah *Ha-motzi* before eating bread. This thanks God for the whole meal. We say a long series of four brakhot called *Birkat Ha-mazon* after eating. In this book we'll only learn one line of *Birkat Ha-mazon*."

Both of these brakhot teach us that we should say a brakhah over any one of the gifts which God has given us. It is a mitzvah to say, "thank you," for anything which gives us pleasure.

בָּרוּךְ אַתָּה יהוה אֱלֹהֵינוּ מֶלֶךְ הָעוֹלָם,

הַמּוֹצִיא לֶחֶם מִן הָאָרֶץ.

Blessed are You, Adonai, Our God, Ruler of the Cosmos,
The One Who-Makes-Bread-Grow-Out of the ground.

בָּרוּךְ אַתָּה יהוה, הַזָּן אֶת הַכֹּל.

Blessed are You, Adonai, The One-Who-Feeds all.

Recitation

Read the following words:

1. הַמּוֹצִיא הַכֹּל הָאָרֶץ אַתָּה מִן
2. בָּרוּךְ הַזָּן בְּמִצְוֹתָיו לֶחֶם אֱלֹהֵינוּ
3. אֶת יהוה אֲשֶׁר הַכֹּל כָּל
4. קָדוֹשׁ הַמּוֹצִיא הַזָּן אֶת הָאָרֶץ
5. אֶחָד בָּרְכוּ הָעוֹלָם הַמְבֹרָךְ לֶחֶם
6. הַמּוֹצִיא נֶאְדָּר הַזָּן מַלְכוּתוֹ שָׁלוֹם

Read these phrases

7. הַמּוֹצִיא לֶחֶם   הַזָּן אֶת הַכֹּל   מִן הָאָרֶץ
8. אֲשֶׁר קִדְּשָׁנוּ   לְהַדְלִיק נֵר   לֶחֶם מִן הָאָרֶץ
9. הָאֵל הַקָּדוֹשׁ   לְעוֹלָם וָעֶד   לְדֹר וָדֹר
10. הַזָּן אֶת הַכֹּל   הַמּוֹצִיא לֶחֶם   מִן הָאָרֶץ

Read these brakhot:

11. בָּרוּךְ אַתָּה יהוה אֱלֹהֵינוּ מֶלֶךְ הָעוֹלָם,
12. הַמּוֹצִיא לֶחֶם מִן הָאָרֶץ.
13. בָּרוּךְ אַתָּה יהוה, הַזָּן אֶת הַכֹּל.

ה = The Definite Article

Think about the meaning of "the." "The" is kind of hard to define, except we know what it really means. "A" thing is different than "The" thing. Consider the difference between being "a winner" and being "the winner." (In English these three letters make a big difference.)

"The" is definite. It is very specific. It makes "a" thing into "the one and only" thing we are considering. That is why we call "the" a Definite Article. In Hebrew we make "a" thing into "the" thing by adding the letter ה as a prefix. (A prefix is something you add onto the beginning of a word.)

Be certain and circle the definite articles found below:

1. מְבֹרָךְ הַמְבֹרָךְ אֶרֶץ הָאָרֶץ
2. אֵל הָאֵל קָדוֹשׁ הַקָּדוֹשׁ
3. מוֹצִיא הַמּוֹצִיא כֹּל הַכֹּל
4. זָן הַזָּן קָדוֹשׁ הַקָּדוֹשׁ
5. עוֹלָם הָעוֹלָם הוּא הַלְלוּיָהּ

Read these brakhot:

6. בָּרוּךְ אַתָּה יהוה אֱלֹהֵינוּ מֶלֶךְ הָעוֹלָם,
7. 
הַמּוֹצִיא לֶחֶם מִן הָאָרֶץ.
8. בָּרוּךְ אַתָּה יהוה, הַזָּן אֶת הַכֹּל.

Dividing Into Parts

Divide the words in these prayers into parts:

1. בָּרוּךְ אַתָּה יהוה אֱלֹהֵינוּ מֶלֶךְ הָעוֹלָם,
2. הַמּוֹצִיא לֶחֶם מִן הָאָרֶץ.
3. הַזָּן אֶת הַכֹּל
4. אֲשֶׁר קִדְּשָׁנוּ בְּמִצְוֹתָיו וְצִוָּנוּ
5. לְהַדְלִיק נֵר שֶׁל שַׁבָּת
6. לְהַדְלִיק נֵר שֶׁל יוֹם טוֹב
7. לְהַדְלִיק נֵר שֶׁל חֲנֻכָּה
8. בָּרוּךְ אַתָּה יהוה אֱלֹהֵינוּ מֶלֶךְ הָעוֹלָם,
9. הַמּוֹצִיא לֶחֶם מִן הָאָרֶץ.
10. בָּרוּךְ אַתָּה יהוה, הַזָּן אֶת הַכֹּל

How does the □ְ help us divide syllables? ______________________________

____

Comprehension

בָּרוּךְ אַתָּה יהוה אֱלֹהֵינוּ מֶלֶךְ הָעוֹלָם,
הַמּוֹצִיא לֶחֶם מִן הָאָרֶץ.

Blessed are You, Adonai, Our God, Ruler of the Cosmos,
The One-Who-Makes-Bread-Grow-Out of the ground.

בָּרוּךְ אַתָּה יהוה, הַזָּן אֶת הַכֹּל.

Blessed are You, Adonai, The One-Who-Feeds all.

1. Circle all the definite articles (ה which means "the").
2. Underline the Hebrew word for "land."
3. Circle the Hebrew word for "bread."
4. Box the Hebrew word for "all."
5. Double underline the Hebrew word for "feed."

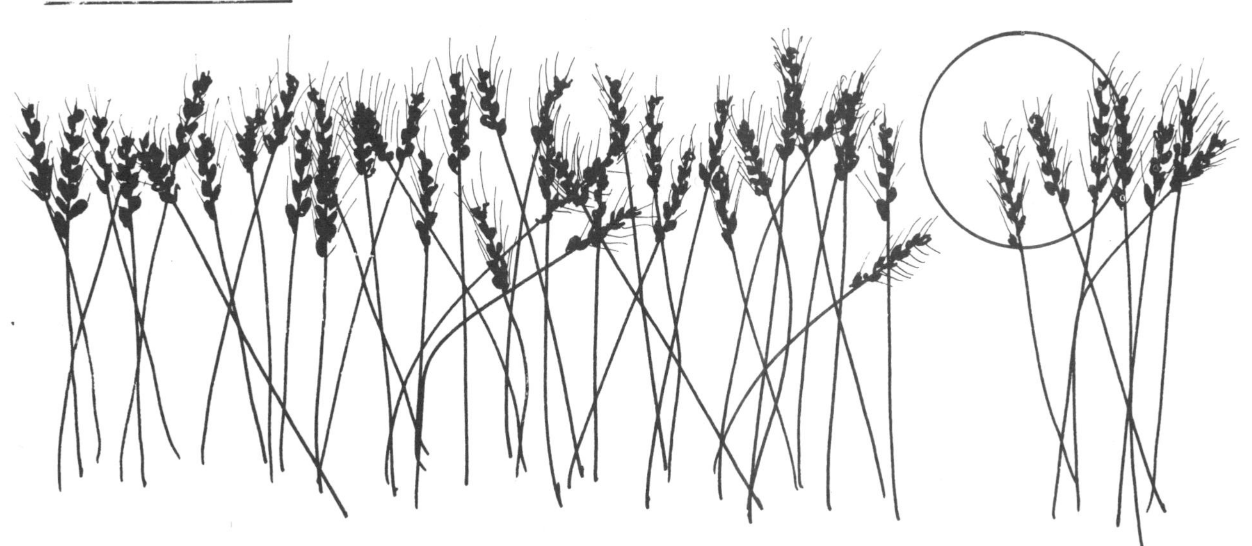

RABBI ABRAHAM, THE RABBI OF APT, WAS OLD AND SICK. STILL, EVERY DAY HIS STUDENTS GATHERED AROUND HIS TABLE TO STUDY.

TABLE, DEAR TABLE, 100 YEARS FROM NOW, WHEN I DIE, I WANT YOU TO BE MY WITNESS.

THAT I LEARNED TO WORRY ABOUT THOSE WHO ARE HUNGRY, BY SAYING A BRAKHAH EVERY TIME I ATE AT YOU.

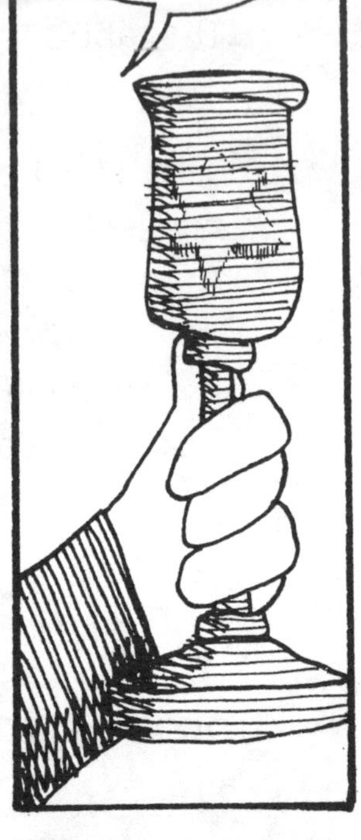

THAT I LEARNED ABOUT HOLINESS WHEN I WELCOMED SHABBAT AT YOU EVERY WEEK.

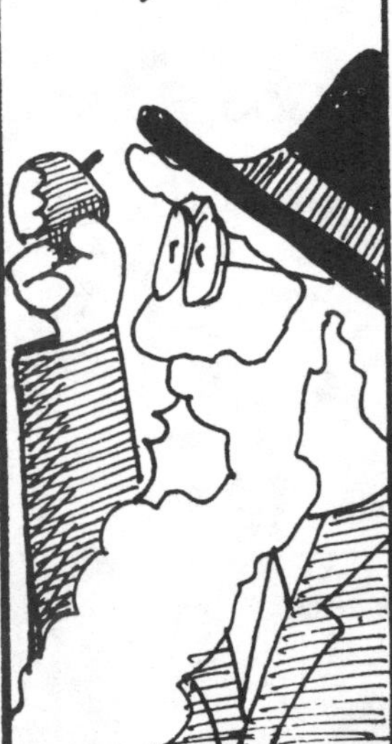

THAT SAYING THE RIGHT BRAKHAH OVER EACH FRUIT AND EACH FOOD I ATE AT YOU, TAUGHT ME HOW MUCH GOD HAS CREATED.

AND THAT I LET THE WORDS OF THE TORAH NOURISH ME, EVERY TIME I STUDIED ON YOU!

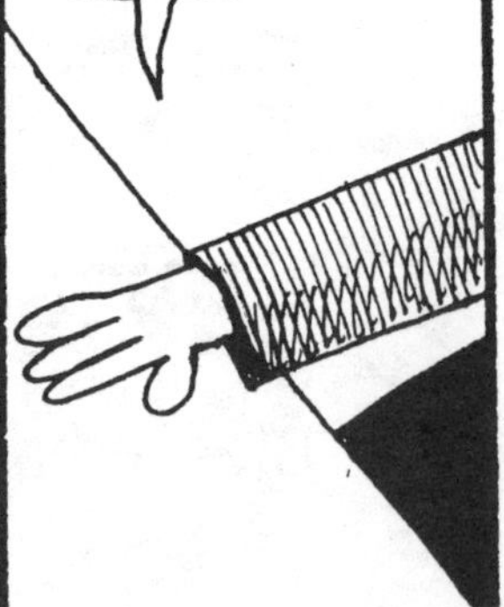

IN FACT, 100 YEARS FROM NOW, I WANT MY COFFIN MADE FROM THIS TABLE.

WITHIN A MONTH THE RABBI WAS DEAD, BUT HIS STUDENTS NEVER FORGOT HIS LAST LESSON.

Vine Fruit, Tree Fruit, and Ground Fruit

The rabbis wrote different brakhot to say before eating every kind of food. Each kind of food has its own brakhah. These different brakhot teach us a lesson.

Before I eat something, I am supposed to say a brakhah and thank God. Before I can say the brakhah, I have to study my food and know where it grew and what is in it. That means I have to know something about nature, about all the things which God created. The different brakhot for different foods make sure that I am really amazed at everything that God created. Once I've really studied it carefully, I really know that the world is a wonderful collection of miracles. Thanks, God.

בָּרוּךְ אַתָּה יהוה אֱלֹהֵינוּ מֶלֶךְ הָעוֹלָם, בּוֹרֵא פְּרִי הַגָּפֶן.

Blessed are You, Adonai, Our God, Ruler of the Cosmos,
The One-Who-Creates the fruit of the vine.

בָּרוּךְ אַתָּה יהוה אֱלֹהֵינוּ מֶלֶךְ הָעוֹלָם, בּוֹרֵא פְּרִי הָעֵץ.

Blessed are You, Adonai, Our God, Ruler of the Cosmos,
The One-Who-Creates the fruit of the tree.

בָּרוּךְ אַתָּה יהוה אֱלֹהֵינוּ מֶלֶךְ הָעוֹלָם, בּוֹרֵא פְּרִי הָאֲדָמָה.

Blessed are You, Adonai, Our God, Ruler of the Cosmos,
The One-Who-Creates the fruit of the ground.

Recitation

Read these words:

1. מֶלֶךְ הַגָּפֶן בָּרוּךְ הָעוֹלָם
2. אַתָּה הוּא בּוֹרֵא יהוה
3. אֱלֹהֵינוּ מִן עָלֵינוּ פְּרִי
4. בְּמִצְוֹתָיו הָאֲדָמָה אֲשֶׁר לְהַדְלִיק
5. הָעֵץ וְצִוָּנוּ קִדְּשָׁנוּ מַלְכוּתוֹ
6. אָמֵן חֲנֻכָּה כָּל שַׁבָּת

Read these brakhot:

7. בָּרוּךְ אַתָּה יהוה אֱלֹהֵינוּ מֶלֶךְ הָעוֹלָם,
בּוֹרֵא פְּרִי הַגָּפֶן.

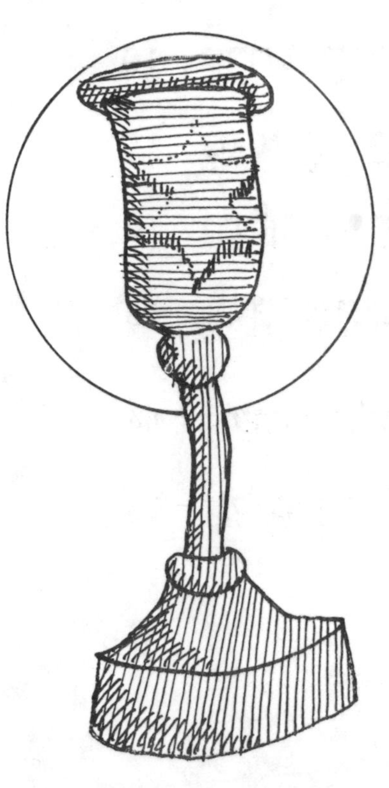

8. בָּרוּךְ אַתָּה יהוה אֱלֹהֵינוּ מֶלֶךְ הָעוֹלָם,
בּוֹרֵא פְּרִי הָעֵץ.

9. בָּרוּךְ אַתָּה יהוה אֱלֹהֵינוּ מֶלֶךְ הָעוֹלָם,
בּוֹרֵא פְּרִי הָאֲדָמָה.

10. בָּרוּךְ אַתָּה יהוה אֱלֹהֵינוּ מֶלֶךְ הָעוֹלָם,
הַמּוֹצִיא לֶחֶם מִן הָאָרֶץ

Review

Read these prayers:

1. בָּרְכוּ אֶת יהוה הַמְבֹרָךְ.
2. בָּרוּךְ יהוה הַמְבֹרָךְ לְעוֹלָם וָעֶד.

3. שְׁמַע יִשְׂרָאֵל, יהוה אֱלֹהֵינוּ יהוה אֶחָד.
4. בָּרוּךְ שֵׁם כְּבוֹד מַלְכוּתוֹ לְעוֹלָם וָעֶד.

5. מִי כָמֹכָה בָּאֵלִם, יהוה
6. מִי־כָּמֹכָה נֶאְדָּר בַּקֹּדֶשׁ,
7. נוֹרָא תְהִלֹּת, עֹשֵׂה פֶלֶא
8. יהוה יִמְלֹךְ לְעוֹלָם וָעֶד.
9. בָּרוּךְ אַתָּה יהוה, גָּאַל יִשְׂרָאֵל.

10. קָדוֹשׁ, קָדוֹשׁ, קָדוֹשׁ יהוה צְבָאוֹת,
11. מְלֹא כָל־הָאָרֶץ כְּבוֹדוֹ.
12. יִמְלֹךְ יהוה לְעוֹלָם, אֱלֹהַיִךְ צִיּוֹן לְדֹר וָדֹר, הַלְלוּיָהּ.
13. בָּרוּךְ אַתָּה יהוה, הָאֵל הַקָּדוֹשׁ.

14. עֹשֶׂה שָׁלוֹם בִּמְרוֹמָיו הוּא יַעֲשֶׂה שָׁלוֹם
15. עָלֵינוּ וְעַל כָּל־יִשְׂרָאֵל, וְאִמְרוּ אָמֵן.

continued on next page.

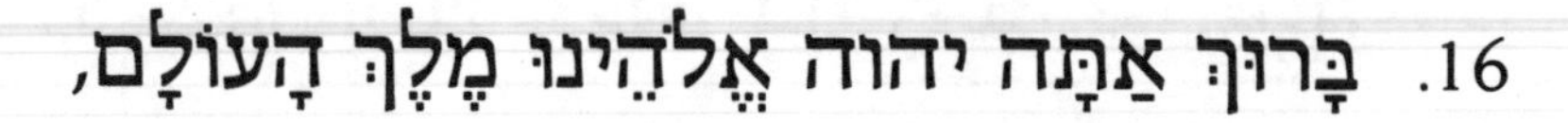

16. בָּרוּךְ אַתָּה יהוה אֱלֹהֵינוּ מֶלֶךְ הָעוֹלָם,

17. אֲשֶׁר קִדְּשָׁנוּ בְּמִצְוֹתָיו וְצִוָּנוּ

18. לְהַדְלִיק נֵר שֶׁל שַׁבָּת.

19. לְהַדְלִיק נֵר שֶׁל יוֹם טוֹב.

20. לְהַדְלִיק נֵר שֶׁל חֲנֻכָּה.

21. בָּרוּךְ אַתָּה יהוה אֱלֹהֵינוּ מֶלֶךְ הָעוֹלָם,

22. הַמּוֹצִיא לֶחֶם מִן הָאָרֶץ.

23. בָּרוּךְ אַתָּה יהוה, הַזָּן אֶת הַכֹּל.

24. בָּרוּךְ אַתָּה יהוה אֱלֹהֵינוּ מֶלֶךְ הָעוֹלָם, בּוֹרֵא פְּרִי הַגָּפֶן.

25. בָּרוּךְ אַתָּה יהוה אֱלֹהֵינוּ מֶלֶךְ הָעוֹלָם, בּוֹרֵא פְּרִי הָעֵץ.

26. בָּרוּךְ אַתָּה יהוה אֱלֹהֵינוּ מֶלֶךְ הָעוֹלָם, בּוֹרֵא פְּרִי הָאֲדָמָה.

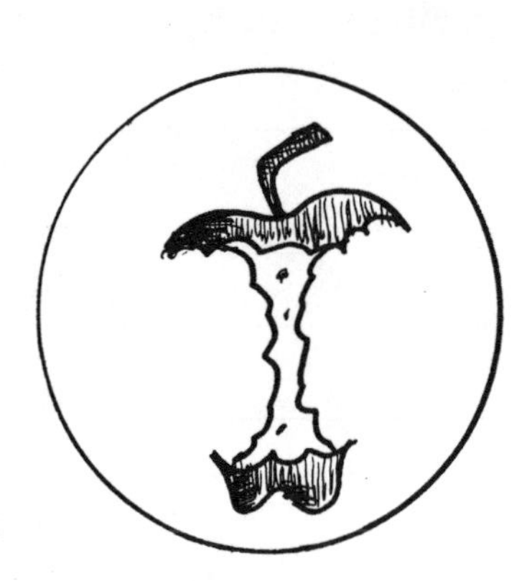

1. Identify the purpose of each prayer.
2. Circle all the words in the בָּרוּךְ family.
3. Box all the words in the מֶלֶךְ family.
4. Underline all the words in the קָדוֹשׁ family.
5. Double underline all the words in the מִצְוָה family.

Comprehension

בָּרוּךְ אַתָּה יהוה אֱלֹהֵינוּ מֶלֶךְ הָעוֹלָם, בּוֹרֵא פְּרִי הַגָּפֶן.

Blessed are You, Adonai, Our God, Ruler of the Cosmos,
The One-Who-Creates the fruit of the vine.

בָּרוּךְ אַתָּה יהוה אֱלֹהֵינוּ מֶלֶךְ הָעוֹלָם, בּוֹרֵא פְּרִי הָעֵץ.

Blessed are You, Adonai, Our God, Ruler of the Cosmos,
The One-Who-Creates the fruit of the tree.

בָּרוּךְ אַתָּה יהוה אֱלֹהֵינוּ מֶלֶךְ הָעוֹלָם, בּוֹרֵא פְּרִי הָאֲדָמָה.

Blessed are You, Adonai, Our God, Ruler of the Cosmos,
The One-Who-Creates the fruit of the ground.

1. Underline the word for "fruit of."
2. Circle the prefixes that mean "the."
3. גֶּפֶן = ______________________

   עֵץ = ______________________

   אֲדָמָה = ______________________

It's Time to Dance
Once, an old man got up and danced. They tried to stop him, but he said:
It's time to dance.
Then he told this story:
Once Rabbi Uri of Strelisk was collecting tzedakah money, he came to Moshe Lev of Sasov.
Tzedakah!
Rabbi Moshe Lev answered him:
I have no money, but I'll dance for you.
The Rabbi of Sasov danced all night.
All night Rabbi Uri watched; in every step was a holy meaning.
At dawn, Rabbi Moshe Lev said:
Wait here, I'll be back with money.
Two days later the Rabbi of Sasov came back.
Years ago, I, too went on a trip to collect tzedakah
a young boy went with me, to show me the way. He was very clever.
It took just a few days to collect the money. I promised him:
I'll dance at your wedding.
CONT.

9.2

The Blessing Over Time

A Question: What do the following have in common: lighting one candle on the H̱anukkiah; having a thirteenth birthday; eating the first peach of the year; going to seder; hearing really good news; or seeing a friend for the first time in thirty days?

Answer: They are all times when we can say the brakhah *she-he-ẖe-yanu*.

The *she-he-ẖe-yanu* is a brakhah over time. It is said at special moments and at special experiences. It is a way of saying, "I am really glad that I am alive and able to have this happen to me. Thanks, God."

בָּרוּךְ אַתָּה יהוה אֱלֹהֵינוּ מֶלֶךְ הָעוֹלָם,

שֶׁהֶחֱיָנוּ וְקִיְּמָנוּ וְהִגִּיעָנוּ לַזְּמַן הַזֶּה.

Blessed are You, Adonai, Our God, Ruler of the Cosmos,
The One-Who-Kept-Us-Alive, Who-Kept-Us-Going, and Who-Led-Us to this very time.

Recitation

Read these words:

1. שֶׁ/הֶ/חֱ/יָ/נוּ   וְ/קִ/יְּ/מָ/נוּ   וְ/הִ/גִּי/עָ/נוּ

2. שֶׁהֶחֱיָנוּ   וְקִיְּמָנוּ   וְהִגִּיעָנוּ   וְהִגִּיעָנוּ
3. וְקִיְּמָנוּ   וְהִגִּיעָנוּ   שֶׁהֶחֱיָנוּ   שֶׁהֶחֱיָנוּ
4. וְהִגִּיעָנוּ   שֶׁהֶחֱיָנוּ   וְקִיְּמָנוּ   וְקִיְּמָנוּ
5. לַזְּמַן   הַזֶּה   לַזְּמַן   הַזֶּה
6. בָּרוּךְ   אַתָּה   יהוה   אֱלֹהֵינוּ
7. מֶלֶךְ   הָעוֹלָם   שֶׁהֶחֱיָנוּ   וְקִיְּמָנוּ
8. וְהִגִּיעָנוּ   לַזְּמַן   הַזֶּה   שֶׁהֶחֱיָנוּ

Read these lines:

9. בָּרוּךְ אַתָּה יהוה אֱלֹהֵינוּ מֶלֶךְ הָעוֹלָם,
10. שֶׁהֶחֱיָנוּ וְקִיְּמָנוּ וְהִגִּיעָנוּ לַזְּמַן הַזֶּה.
11. בָּרוּךְ אַתָּה יהוה אֱלֹהֵינוּ מֶלֶךְ הָעוֹלָם,
12. שֶׁהֶחֱיָנוּ וְקִיְּמָנוּ וְהִגִּיעָנוּ לַזְּמַן הַזֶּה.

A Common Suffix

Read these words:

1. אֱלֹהֵינוּ מַלְכֵּנוּ עָלֵינוּ קִדְּשָׁנוּ

2. שֶׁהֶחֱיָנוּ וְקִיְּמָנוּ וְהִגִּיעָנוּ

What do they all have in common? ______________________________

__________ means "we/our/us."

Match the base words:

שֶׁהֶחֱיָנוּ	הִגִּיעַ = Arrive
וְקִיְּמָנוּ	חַי = Life
וְהִגִּיעָנוּ	קָיָם = To keep going

Explain each of these words.

Dividing Into Parts

1. Divide the שֶׁהֶחֱיָנוּ into syllables:

1. בָּרוּךְ אַתָּה יהוה
2. אֱלֹהֵינוּ מֶלֶךְ הָעוֹלָם
3. שֶׁהֶחֱיָנוּ
4. וְקִיְּמָנוּ
5. וְהִגִּיעָנוּ
6. לַזְּמַן הַזֶּה.

2. Go back and practice Exercises 8.4–5.

Comprehension

בָּרוּךְ אַתָּה יהוה אֱלֹהֵינוּ מֶלֶךְ הָעוֹלָם

שֶׁהֶחֱיָנוּ וְקִיְּמָנוּ וְהִגִּיעָנוּ לַזְּמַן הַזֶּה.

Blessed are You, Adonai, Our God, Ruler of the Cosmos,
The One-Who-Kept-Us-Alive, Who-Kept-Us-Going,
and Who-Led-Us to this very time.

1. Circle every "ה" which is a definite article ("the").
2. Underline the נוּ endings which mean "we/our/us."
3. Box the Hebrew words which mean "this time."
4. Double box the Hebrew word which means "Who-Kept-Us-Going."
5. Double circle the Hebrew word which means "Who-Kept-Us-Alive."
6. Double underline the word which means "Who-Led-Us."

THE HOLY YEHUDI ONCE TOLD RABBI BUNAM TO TAKE A JOURNEY.

HE LEFT TOWN WITH A GROUP OF HASIDIM.

NEAR NOON, THEY CAME TO A INN.

IT IS AN HONOR TO WELCOME SUCH A PIOUS GROUP TO OUR INN.

WOULD YOU PLEASE BE MY GUESTS FOR LUNCH?

RABBI BUNAM SAT DOWN IN THE DINING ROOM WHILE THE REST OF THE HASIDIM WENT INTO THE KITCHEN TO CHECK OUT THE FOOD.

HOW KOSHER IS THIS?
WHO DID THE INSPECTION?
WAS THE ANIMAL PERFECT?

SUDDENLY, A MAN WHO WAS DRESSED IN RAGS SAID:

YOU MAKE A BIG TO-DO ABOUT THE HOLINESS OF WHAT YOU PUT IN YOUR MOUTHS.

IT WOULD BE GOOD IF YOU CARED AS MUCH ABOUT THE HOLINESS OF WHAT CAME OUT OF THEM.

IN THE NEXT INSTANT THE MAN WAS GONE. RABBI BUNAM SMILED AND UNDERSTOOD.

The Four Questions: The Introduction

Read this question:

1. מַה נִּשְׁתַּנָּה הַלַּיְלָה הַזֶּה מִכָּל הַלֵּילוֹת?

What are the differences between this night and all other nights?

At the Pesaḫ Seder, the youngest child stands up and asks four questions. Actually, if you count, there are five of the four questions. The first of the four questions, the one found on this page, is really an introduction. It asks why we do all these special things at a seder meal—instead of just having a regular dinner.

Read these words:

2. הַלַּיְלָה   הַלֵּילוֹת   מַה   כָּל

3. נִשְׁתַּנָּה   מִכָּל   הַזֶּה   הַלֵּילוֹת

4. מַה   הַזֶּה   נִשְׁתַּנָּה   מִכָּל

5. לַיְלָה   הַלַּיְלָה   הַלֵּילוֹת   הַזֶּה

6. מַה נִּשְׁתַּנָּה הַלַּיְלָה הַזֶּה מִכָּל הַלֵּילוֹת?

1. Box the Hebrew word which means "all."
2. Underline the Hebrew word which means "this."
3. Circle each ה which means "the."
4. The Hebrew word מִן means "from." It can also be shortened to a one-letter prefix (a letter stuck on the beginning of a word). Box that prefix.
5. The word for "night" appears in two different forms (singular and plural). Circle them both.

The Four Questions: Question 1

Read this question:

1. שֶׁבְּכָל הַלֵּילוֹת אָנוּ אוֹכְלִין חָמֵץ וּמַצָּה
2. הַלַּיְלָה הַזֶּה כֻּלּוֹ מַצָּה.

On all other nights we eat both *ẖametz* and *matzah*. On this night, all is *matzah*.

On the page before this, we had the introductory question. It noted that seder night is very different from all other nights. Now, in each of the four questions, we will look at one of those differences.

The first question asks about *matzah*. *Matzah* is a special bread which has been made very quickly so that the dough will not have time to rise. At Pesaẖ, and at the seder, we eat only *matzah*.

H̱ametz is any food which is made from grain which has been allowed to rise. At Pesaẖ, Jews are not allowed to own or use *H̱ametz*.

Read these words:

3. הַלֵּילוֹת   מַצָּה   וּמַצָּה   אוֹכְלִין
4. הַזֶּה   חָמֵץ   שֶׁבְּכָל   הַלַּיְלָה
5. כֻּלּוֹ   שֶׁבְּכָל   אָנוּ   מַצָּה
6. חָמֵץ   אוֹכְלִין   כֻּלּוֹ   הַזֶּה

7. שֶׁבְּכָל הַלֵּילוֹת אָנוּ אוֹכְלִין חָמֵץ וּמַצָּה

8. הַלַּיְלָה הַזֶּה כֻּלּוֹ מַצָּה?

1. Circle the Hebrew words for "unleavened bread."
2. Box the Hebrew word for "grain products which have risen."
3. Star☆ the word which means "we." Clue: look at the suffix.
4. Double underline the Hebrew words for "night" and "nights."
5. The Hebrew word _____ means "all." Circle the two Hebrew words which have it as a "base word."
6. Which word means "this?" ______________________________

10.4

The Four Questions: Question 2

The second question asks about *maror*. *Maror* is the bitter herb. At the Pesah Seder we make a point of eating bitter herbs twice. Once we eat them with *haroset* and say a brakhah over them. The second time we sandwich them with *matzah* and make a "Hillel Sandwich."

This question asks why we make a special deal out of *maror*.

Read this question:

1. שֶׁבְּכָל הַלֵּילוֹת אָנוּ אוֹכְלִין שְׁאָר יְרָקוֹת

2. הַלַּיְלָה הַזֶּה מָרוֹר.

On all other nights we eat both *hametz* and *matzah*. On this night, all is *matzah*.
On all other nights we eat any kind of vegetables. On this night, *maror*.

Read these words.

3. הַזֶּה מָרוֹר אוֹכְלִין יְרָקוֹת אָנוּ

4. הַלַּיְלָה הַלֵּילוֹת שְׁאָר יְרָקוֹת מָרוֹר

5. שֶׁבְּכָל הַלֵּילוֹת אָנוּ אוֹכְלִין חָמֵץ וּמַצָּה,

6. הַלַּיְלָה הַזֶּה כֻּלּוֹ מַצָּה.

7. שֶׁבְּכָל הַלֵּילוֹת אָנוּ אוֹכְלִין שְׁאָר יְרָקוֹת,

8. הַלַּיְלָה הַזֶּה מָרוֹר.

1. Box the Hebrew word for "bitter herb."
2. Circle the Hebrew words which mean "night" and "nights."
3. Underline the Hebrew words which mean "eat." (They are part of the אוֹכֵל family).
4. Double underline the Hebrew words which mean "we."
5. Star the words built on the "base-word" כָּל.
6. Put two boxes around the Hebrew words which mean "this."

The Four Questions: Question 3

At a regular meal we do things like dip french fries in ketchup and fish sticks into tartar sauce. At a Aeder meal we also dip, but we make it part of the ceremony. It isn't a matter of taste—it is a matter of tradition. At the Seder we dip the parsley or other vegetables in salt water and the *maror* in the *ẖaroset*. This question asks, "Why do we make a ritual out of these two dippings?"

Read this question:

1. שֶׁבְּכָל הַלֵּילוֹת אֵין אָנוּ מַטְבִּילִין אֲפִילוּ פַּעַם אֶחָת,
2. הַלַּיְלָה הַזֶּה שְׁתֵּי פְעָמִים?

On all other nights we don't even dip (as a ritual) even once—
this night (we dip) two times (and both of them are part of the ceremony).

Read these words.

3. הַלֵּילוֹת אֵין פַּעַם פְּעָמִים הַזֶּה
4. הַלַּיְלָה שְׁתֵּי אֶחָד אֶחָת אֲפִילוּ
5. מַטְבִּילִין אָנוּ מַצָּה חָמֵץ שֶׁבְּכָל
6. שֶׁבְּכָל הַלֵּילוֹת הַלַּיְלָה הַזֶּה
7. שְׁתֵּי פְעָמִים פַּעַם אֶחָת
8. מַטְבִּילִין אֲפִילוּ פַּעַם אֶחָת, הַלַּיְלָה הַזֶּה שְׁתֵּי פְעָמִים

9. שֶׁבְּכָל הַלֵּילוֹת אֵין אָנוּ מַטְבִּילִין אֲפִילוּ פַּעַם אֶחָת

10. הַלַּיְלָה הַזֶּה שְׁתֵּי פְעָמִים.

1. Underline the Hebrew words for "night" and "nights."
2. (Circle) the feminine version of the word אֶחָד.
3. [Box] the words in the פַּעַם family. It means "a time" or "a turn."
4. Star the Hebrew word for "we."

10.6

The Four Questions: Question 4

One Seder custom is to use cushions or even a sofa instead of a regular chair. We recline (sort of lay down) at a Seder meal. It is a way of feeling really free. This question asks about that custom.

Read this question:

1. שֶׁבְּכָל הַלֵּילוֹת אָנוּ אוֹכְלִין בֵּין יוֹשְׁבִין וּבֵין מְסֻבִּין,

2. הַלַּיְלָה הַזֶּה כֻּלָּנוּ מְסֻבִּין.

On all other nights we eat sometimes sitting and sometimes reclining. This night all of us recline.

Read all of the questions.

1. מַה נִּשְׁתַּנָּה הַלַּיְלָה הַזֶּה מִכָּל הַלֵּילוֹת?
2. שֶׁבְּכָל הַלֵּילוֹת אָנוּ אוֹכְלִין חָמֵץ וּמַצָּה
3. הַלַּיְלָה הַזֶּה כֻּלּוֹ מַצָּה.
4. שֶׁבְּכָל הַלֵּילוֹת אָנוּ אוֹכְלִין שְׁאָר יְרָקוֹת
5. הַלַּיְלָה הַזֶּה מָרוֹר.
6. שֶׁבְּכָל הַלֵּילוֹת אֵין אָנוּ מַטְבִּילִין אֲפִילוּ פַּעַם אֶחָת
7. הַלַּיְלָה הַזֶּה שְׁתֵּי פְעָמִים.
8. שֶׁבְּכָל הַלֵּילוֹת אָנוּ אוֹכְלִין בֵּין יוֹשְׁבִין וּבֵין מְסֻבִּין
9. הַלַּיְלָה הַזֶּה כֻּלָּנוּ מְסֻבִּין.

What are the differences between this night and all other nights?
On all other nights we eat both hametz and *matzah*. On this night, all is *matzah*.
On all other nights we eat any kind of vegetables. On this night, *maror*.
On all other nights we don't dip (as a ritual) even once—
this night (we dip) two times (and both of them are part of the ceremony).
On all other nights we eat sometimes sitting and sometimes reclining. This night all of us recline.

1. Box the word for "recline."
2. Circle the word for "sit."
3. Underline all the words built from the base-word "אוֹכֵל."
4. Double underline the Hebrew word for "eat."
5. Put one star over the Hebrew word for "bitter herbs."
6. Put two stars over the Hebrew word for "unleavened bread."
7. Put three stars over the Hebrew word for "grain product which has risen."
8. Double box all the Hebrew words which mean "night" or "nights."
4. Star the Hebrew word for "we."